The
ELEPHANT
SCIENTIST

Text copyright © 2011 by Caitlin O'Connell and Donna M. Jackson

Photo credits appear on page iv. All other photographs copyright © 2011 by Caitlin O'Connell and Timothy Rodwell

Houghton Mifflin Books for Children is an imprint of Houghton Mifflin Harcourt Publishing Company.

www.hmhbooks.com

The text of this book is set in Meridien.
Book design by YAY! Design.

Library of Congress Cataloging-in-Publication Data

O'Connell, Caitlin, 1965–

The elephant scientist / by Caitlin O'Connell and Donna M. Jackson; photographs by Caitlin O'Connell and Timothy Rodwell.
    p. cm.
ISBN 978-0-547-05344-8
    1. African elephant—Namibia—Juvenile literature.
    2. African elephant—Behavior—Research—Juvenile literature.
    3. O'Connell, Caitlin, 1965—Juvenile literature.
    I. Jackson, Donna M., 1959–.
    II. Rodwell, T. C., ill.
    III. Title.

QL737.P98O257 2011
599.67'4096881—dc22

2010014134

Manufactured in the U.S.A.

WOZ 10 9 8 7 6 5 4 3 2

4500347743

With love to Peter, the lone "bull" in our herd. —D.M.J.

To my godson, Connor, for whom I named the elephant Congo Connor, inspired by his confidence, his physical and mental agility, and his casual cool among his peers and elders. —C.O.C.

ELEPHANT
The SCIENTIST

by Caitlin O'Connell and Donna M. Jackson

Photographs by Caitlin O'Connell and Timothy Rodwell

Houghton Mifflin Books for Children
Houghton Mifflin Harcourt
Boston   New York   2011

ACKNOWLEDGMENTS

I'd like to thank all of my colleagues who worked on this study over the years, in particular, my husband, Timothy Rodwell; my current master's student, Colleen Kinzley; my former postdoc, Jason Wood; and my former and current mentors on this research, Lynette Hart, Byron Arnason, Simon Klemperer, Sunil Puria, Rob Jackler, and Robert Sapolsky, as well as Sam Wasser and his lab at the University of Washington for hormone and genetic analysis, and all the hard-working students from Stanford University and University of Namibia. Financial or in-kind support for this research came from Stanford University, the Oakland Zoo, Scheide Fund, Seaver Foundation, Noldus software, Soltec Namibia, and the Utopia Scientific paying volunteer program. I also thank the Ministry of Environment and Tourism for ground support and the Namibia Nature Foundation for administrative support. Last but most important thanks goes to my coauthor, Donna Jackson, for brainstorming the idea for this book with me and creating an avenue to make it happen. —C.O.C.

Many thanks to Caitlin O'Connell and Timothy Rodwell for sharing their valuable research and exquisite images in the book—it's a privilege to tell your story. I'm also grateful to Colleen Kinzley, general curator at the Oakland Zoo, for sharing her work and introducing me to Donna the elephant, as well as to researcher Joyce Poole, director, ElephantVoices, for taking time to share her insights on elephant conservation.

A special note of appreciation to Ann Rider for embracing the book and guiding us through the pages, and to Charlie Jackson, who cheerfully trumpets through the seasons. — D.M.J.

Caitlin and bull elephant at sunset.

PHOTO CREDITS

Table of Contents: Caitlin with elephants and binoculars. Photo by Max Salomon. Copyright © Max Salomon, 2006

Page 4: Young Caitlin with goat, courtesy of the O'Connell family

Page 20: Caitlin with farmers and ranger, courtesy of Ron Connor

Page 30: CT scan, courtesy of John Hutchinson, Ph.D., Royal Veterinary College, University of London

Page 38: Setting up camp, courtesy of Sarah Mesnick, Ph.D., Southwest Fisheries Science Center, NOAA (National Oceanic and Atmospheric Administration), San Diego, California

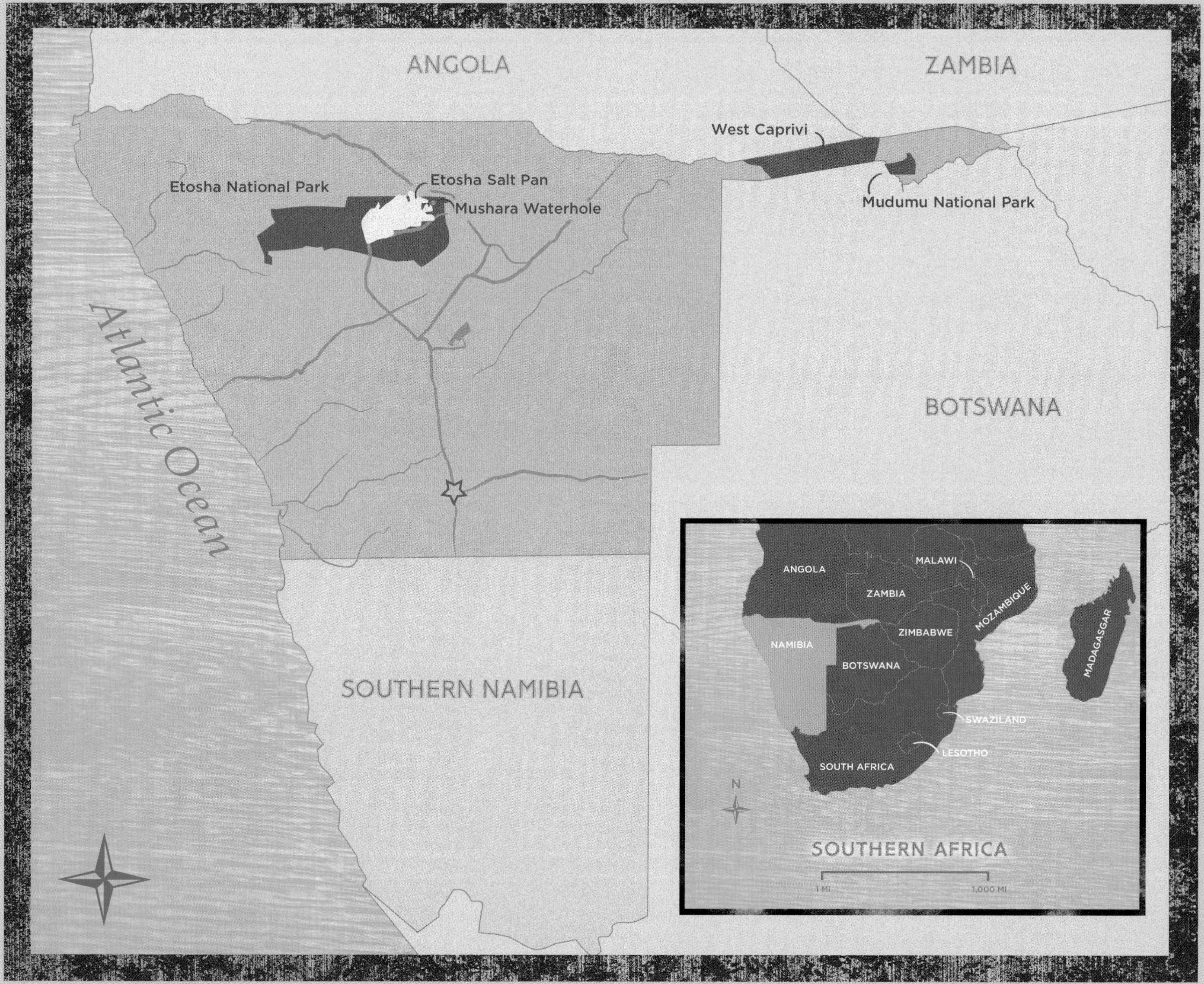
ANGOLA
ZAMBIA
West Caprivi
Etosha National Park
Etosha Salt Pan
Mushara Waterhole
Mudumu National Park
BOTSWANA
Atlantic Ocean
SOUTHERN NAMIBIA
ANGOLA
MALAWI
ZAMBIA
MOZAMBIQUE
ZIMBABWE
NAMIBIA
BOTSWANA
MADAGASGAR
SWAZILAND
LESOTHO
SOUTH AFRICA
N
SOUTHERN AFRICA
1 MI
1,000 MI

CONTENTS

Perseverance and gentleness prevail.
The proper balance of confidence and humility repeatedly leads to triumph.

—Nicholas Fox Weber, reflecting on the character of Babar the Elephant in
The Art of Babar: The Work of Jean and Laurent de Brunhoff

UNEARTHING ELEPHANT SECRETS

Caitlin O'Connell peered through her binoculars and spotted an elephant family walking in the distance. Suddenly, the leader stopped in its tracks. The elephant matriarch—the oldest and wisest female of the group—stood still, shifted her weight, and leaned forward on her front feet. At times the elephant would lift a foot or flatten her trunk on the ground, seeming to concentrate on something. As the mighty matriarch scanned the African horizon, the other elephants followed suit, stopping midstride and standing as still as statues in the sprawling scrub desert of Etosha National Park.

During one sunset Caitlin O'Connell watches for elephants from the top of the bunker at Mushara waterhole in Etosha National Park in Namibia.

An elephant matriarch, below, cautiously leads her family group to water. Sometimes it takes hours for a matriarch to deem it safe to enter the open area of the waterhole.

1

An elephant matriarch stops to ensure it's safe to approach a waterhole. Along with scanning with her ears and smelling with her trunk, she sometimes stands still and leans forward on her front feet—as if listening to something in the ground.

Caitlin watched the scene from a ten-foot-square cement bunker near Mushara waterhole—a popular drinking site for animals that was named after a tree common to the area. The American scientist, who had traveled to Namibia (na-MIH-bee-uh) to study elephants in their natural habitats, couldn't believe what she was seeing.

"I immediately recognized the behavior pattern," says Caitlin. "I had seen this specific sequence of actions while studying the mating calls of much smaller animals known as planthoppers—tiny insects that send signals to each other by vibrating plants with their limbs. When a male planthopper hears the vibrational love call of a female, he freezes in place so he can focus and listen to the message. He'll stop, press down on his legs, move forward, and shift directions," she says. "Then he'll freeze again and press down and listen with his feet."

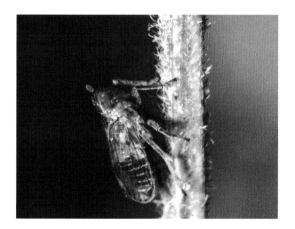

A Hawaiian planthopper straddles a leaf stem in this magnified view. Planthoppers transmit their calls through their feet and into the plant as vibrations.

Studies show that many small animals—from spiders and scorpions to insects and frogs—communicate by vibrating objects in their environment, such as plants, leaves, twigs, and the ground itself. These vibrations are called seismic signals when transmitted through the ground and are so low in frequency that most humans can't hear them, or, in this case, feel them. Once generated, however, the vibrational messages ripple across surfaces like waves on water and ultimately help animals find mates, locate prey, and establish territories. For example, "the male fiddler crab bangs territorial warnings into the sand with its oversized claw," writes Alan Burdick in *Natural History* magazine. "A blind mole rat pounds its head against the walls of its underground tunnels" to ensure its neighbor rats know his territory.

After watching the elephants freeze in unison, Caitlin excitedly recalled her insect studies. Could it be that the giant mammals were sending and receiving messages through the ground like the little planthoppers? Scientists already knew elephants communicated over long distances through low-frequency rumbles that rolled through the air, but was it also possible the animals were talking—and listening—to one another with their feet?

If so, the discovery would be a major breakthrough in decoding some of the mystery surrounding elephant communication. It might help answer questions such as how the animals seem to "sense" rainstorms hundreds of miles away. "It could be that they feel vibrations from the distant thunder with their feet," says Caitlin. Not only would this knowledge help scientists better understand elephants and vibrational communication in general, but it might also help conservationists protect elephants in the wild by understanding how far they might be able to keep in touch with one another and how they may sense their environment.

SLIPPERY BEGINNINGS

Caitlin grew up surrounded by wildlife, but she also had many pets—including a goat and her two kids.

4

C aitlin O'Connell studies elephants today, but her first animal of choice was small, wet, and slimy. Growing up in a forested area of New Jersey—with a pond and several streams—she blissfully spied on all sorts of wildlife, from turtles to snakes.

The frog, however, was her favorite.

"I liked frogs because I could observe them easily," she says. "I could sneak up on them, catch them, and then put them back in the water." Caitlin was also captivated by their different forms. "I was fascinated with tadpoles and enjoyed watching them grow and change—first with their legs popping out and then their tails shrinking. This was my first experience with vibration detection, as I was aware that frogs could detect the vibrations created by my footsteps. I tried to step lightly when approaching the water so that the frogs wouldn't disappear before I had the chance to catch them. I also enjoyed watching them move from water to land," she says. "It's something really special to be able to observe over time."

Caitlin met an abandoned elephant calf at Etosha National Park in 1992 when her research began. It's uncertain why the calf's mother died, but she may have contracted anthrax, which is a naturally occurring disease in the region, or she could have been poached outside the park. Unfortunately, the calf died despite around-the-clock veterinary care.

Caitlin's early observational skills and love of animals have served her well through the years. As an elephant scientist, she relies on patience and perseverance to identify and measure the social behaviors of the majestic mammal.

The third of four children—she has two brothers and a sister—Caitlin credits her psychiatrist dad with introducing her to the natural world. "He would show us the jack-in-the-pulpits and all the flowers that would bloom in the spring, and point out the different animal species that we'd see on a walk," she says. Caitlin's mother, who is an artist, helped her appreciate the world by paying attention to the details. She would show Caitlin how to draw a violet or a pinecone. She also taught her how to mix colors and shapes so Caitlin could paint the plant life and animals she saw around her.

Teachers encouraged Caitlin's talents, as well. "I was quiet in school, but my teachers recognized I was really good at science," she says. The early attention bolstered Caitlin's confidence so much that she took every science course she could in high school and majored in biology and premed in college. Unlike many of her peers, however, Caitlin wasn't certain about going to medical school and becoming a doctor. "While I was fascinated by medicine, I was more interested in animal behavior and the world of field biology," she says. Field biologists study nature and living organisms in their natural habitats. In keeping with her objectives, Caitlin volunteered on a variety of field projects after college—including one involving insects.

"I wasn't necessarily drawn to insects per se," she says, "although I did have a fascination for the miniature. When I saw these amazing animals under magnification, I was hooked. What further intrigued me, however, was the field biologists' passion for these bizarre and curious creatures—so much so that I eventually pursued a master's degree in entomology at the University of Hawaii at Manoa."

Using a needle glued to an old gramophone stylus, Caitlin recorded the vibrational calls of planthoppers and amplified the vibrations so that she could listen to and study their patterns. The process is similar to having a record player stylus read the grooves in a vinyl record and amplifying them to hear the music. "Planthopper mating calls are created within a little drum that sits between their thorax and abdomen," Caitlin explains. "The drum pops in and out—

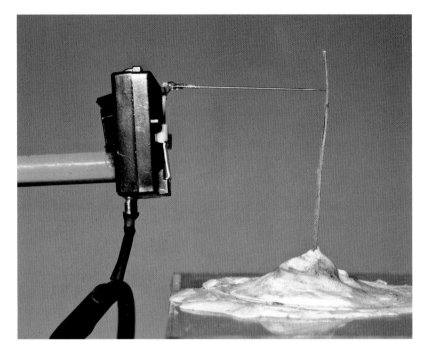

In her planthopper studies, Caitlin recorded the insects' call vibrations and amplified the sounds so that she could listen to them and study their patterns. Since planthoppers are only several millimeters long, the singing male can't be seen in this image.

much like the popping of an empty tin can when you squeeze its sides—and the vibrations from this popping drum travel down through the planthopper's feet and into the plant stem." Biologists estimate that more than 200,000 insect species communicate using vibrational signals. Little did Caitlin know how important this knowledge would be as she entered the next phase of her animal studies.

CALL OF THE WILD

Caitlin worked as a volunteer at Etosha National Park before taking a contract job as an elephant researcher.

After working with planthoppers in graduate school, Caitlin received a rare opportunity to study wild elephants in Africa—a dream come true for the scientist. "I'd always wanted to study large mammals," she says, "but I never imagined I'd have the chance to study nature's largest land mammal." In 1992, she and her now husband, Dr. Tim Rodwell, began a yearlong trip to Africa, where they planned to view wild animals in their natural settings. While on their journey, they volunteered to help with several animal-related research projects and ended up at Etosha National Park. In a welcome twist of fate, the head of research at Etosha offered the couple a three-year job studying elephant movements, habitat, behavior, and interactions with people. "The job

Elephants migrate south from the Caprivi, an area in northeastern Namibia, at the first sign of rain.

involved working in the Caprivi, an area in northeastern Namibia and one of the last places where elephants still migrate hundreds of miles during the wet, or rainy, season." Unfortunately, it's also a place where humans and elephants regularly clash over resources. Soon Caitlin learned what an enormous challenge it was for elephants and farmers to share land and access to water in an open habitat—an area with no fences between national parks and farms.

One problem stems from the elephants' need for ample terrain. Nature has designed them to travel great distances for food and water, with some animals migrating more than three hundred miles each year. These long treks not only allow elephants to satisfy their huge appetites, but also help to spread the seeds of important trees, such as many of the acacias, which have evolved to pass through the elephant's gut before being able to grow. In very dense forests, elephant movements are important because they help knock down trees and open the way for new plants that can be eaten by smaller animals. But when elephants are confined to small areas and aren't able to move along their historic migratory routes, they often overuse the land. This makes it difficult for trees to recover from injuries—such as debarked and broken limbs—and eventually could limit the animals' food supply.

In open habitats such as the Caprivi, where few boundaries exist, some farms sit on the edges of forests where the elephants live. "Since corn is much tastier and easier to eat than tree bark and branches, elephants often wander into farmers' cornfields before harvest time and have a feast," Caitlin says. Sometimes, they'll eat a whole year's worth of a family's food in a single night. As a result, local farmers get

FACING PAGE: At the end of the dry season, there is so little left to eat that large groups of elephants migrate toward greener vegetation at the first sign of rain.

RIGHT: Historically, elephant populations were less compressed and moved freely through regions, occasionally knocking down trees. When too many elephants are limited to a small area, they can destroy trees that are thousands of years old in a short time. During the three years Caitlin worked in the area pictured, she observed this baobab tree being eaten and finally knocked down by the elephants.

A small group of elephants is pursued by helicopter and isolated on the floodplain so scientists can dart and collar a family member and learn more about the elephants' movement patterns.

The researcher Tim Rodwell places a satellite collar on an elephant with the help of the Namibian Ministry of Environment and Tourism game capture team.

angry at having to share space with the elephants. "Our assignment, funded by the Namibian Ministry of Environment and Tourism," says Caitlin, "was to look for ways to keep elephants from eating farmers' crops. Tim would study elephant movements and populations, and I would focus on elephant behaviors, ecology (their relationships with the environment), and their interactions with farmers."

The task was a daunting one, since the scientists hadn't worked with elephants before and had much to learn. Whereas Caitlin's background was in animal communication, her studies were closely tied to their inborn traits. For example, because of the genes it inherited, an insect might produce a particular type of signal to attract a mate. Since elephants are especially intelligent, their behaviors are more complex and can be influenced by many factors besides heredity, such as specific relationships, seniority, and even prior experience. This complexity makes their actions harder to interpret. Despite her different experiences, however, Caitlin hoped to apply a fresh perspective to the field and move it forward in some way.

The scientist began her new role by collecting information from park rangers and reading everything she could about elephants—including their biology, social structure, communication, behaviors, ecology, and feeding habits. What she discovered next about their mechanisms of communication both amazed and bonded her to her elephant subjects in ways she never anticipated.

LIVING LARGE

TOP: An elephant bull (center) escorts a family group to the water. Notice how the elephant bull towers over the females.

ABOVE: A baby elephant fits under its mother's belly for up to a year after birth.

African elephants reign as the largest living land mammals in the world. Adult males, called bulls, typically weigh up to 14,000 pounds, and adult females, called cows, average about 7,000 pounds. The largest African elephant on record weighed an estimated 24,000 pounds—twelve tons—and stood thirteen feet high at his shoulders. That's about twice as tall as the average professional basketball player in America. Newborn elephants, called calves, tip the scales at anywhere from 110 to 260 pounds and stand at about three feet tall at the shoulders. Despite their enormous size, however, some elephants have been clocked running as fast as fifteen miles an hour, which is about the average top speed of physically fit men.

To survive in the wild, elephants eat a healthy mix of foliage and may drink between thirty and fifty gallons of water a day—sometimes all in one drinking session, says Caitlin. The plant-eating pachyderms (a term used for elephants that refers to their thick skin) dine on an average of 250 to 450 pounds of vegetation daily. Grass makes up part of their diet during the

LEFT: A thirsty elephant family group helps itself to a cool drink on a hot afternoon. An adult male elephant can fit at least nine and a half quarts (nine liters) of water in its trunk.

ABOVE: Elephants eat everything from grass to tree bark. When an elephant severely strips a tree of its bark, it eventually kills the tree.

BELOW: It takes a baby elephant several months to gain control of its trunk.

RIGHT: An elephant uses its trunk to assess its environment, sometimes reaching high into the air to smell a suspicious object.

rainy season, but elephants also eat shrubs, twigs, buds, pods, fruits, vegetables, shoots, roots, and tree bark.

Helping find all that food is an elephant's versatile trunk—a unique appendage among living mammals. Comprising more than 40,000 muscles, this long fusion of nose and upper lip helps an elephant breathe, smell, drink, and explore objects. It's so powerful that it can uproot a tree, yet nimble enough to grasp a nut or a berry, says Caitlin. When swimming, an elephant uses its trunk as a snorkel to take in and release air. Elephants also use their trunk to play, fight, comfort, and communicate with one another.

ABOVE LEFT: Elephants use their trunk to dig holes for salt, and wells for water. Salt is an important part of an elephant's diet, especially in hot climates, because it helps them keep water in their bodies.

LEFT: Elephants greet one another by placing their trunk in each other's mouth. This important ritual is similar to a handshake.

ABOVE: Elephants learn the "trunk to mouth" greeting at a very young age.

Elephants use their trunk to rescue others from danger. In this case, a mother and sister come to the aid of a small calf that has fallen into a drinking trough.

Along with its trunk, an elephant's tusks aid in its daily quest for green cuisine. The spearlike extensions allow elephants to dig for food and water and to rip the bark from trees. Tusks are giant incisor teeth made of dentin or ivory—the same material that forms our teeth. They grow throughout an elephant's life and can extend as long as eight feet and weigh more than two hundred pounds. In hostile situations, elephants use their tusks to fight with other elephants or to defend themselves and their calves against predators. Sadly, some people kill elephants for their tusks so that they can sell the ivory illegally. "A poor villager might do this for as little as five dollars of profit," says Caitlin.

When left to live out their natural lives, elephants generally grow to be about sixty-five years old. "It all depends on when they lose their teeth," explains Caitlin. Elephants grow six sets of teeth during their lifetime, with one to two molars in place on each side of the top and bottom jaw at any one time. New teeth erupt at the back of the jaw and push the older ones forward. When the last set of teeth wears out and drops out of an elephant's mouth, the elephant goes hungry and dies because it isn't able to chew and consume enough food.

Tim Rodwell measures the length and number of teeth in this jaw of an elephant bull that lived to be in his forties. While this calculation is impossible on live elephants (unless a plaster cast is made on an anesthetized elephant), it's the most accurate way to determine an animal's age.

Most people know about Asian elephants (*Elephas maximus*) and African elephants (*Loxodonta africana*). But for a while, one species managed to slip by. Scientists now divide African elephants into two subspecies—the African savannah or bush elephant and the smaller African forest elephant. They also divide Asian elephants into four subspecies: Indian, Sri Lankan, Sumatran, and Borneo.

Asian elephants have relatively small ears, a dome-shaped back, and one finger-like projection at the end of their trunk that helps them grasp objects. African elephants, on the other hand, have large ears shaped like the African continent, a concave back, and two fingerlike projections at the tip of their trunk that allow them to pinch and pick up small items. Asian elephants live in places such as India, Sri Lanka, Thailand, Myanmar, Laos, and southern China, where they browse in tropical and subtropical forests. African elephants—the kind that Caitlin primarily studies—dwell in varying densities in the north, east, west, center, and south of Africa, where they stroll grassy savannahs, forests, and open woodlands.

Asian elephants have smaller ears than African elephants and one "finger" at the end of their trunk instead of two. Only the males have tusks.

17

SENSITIVE SOULS

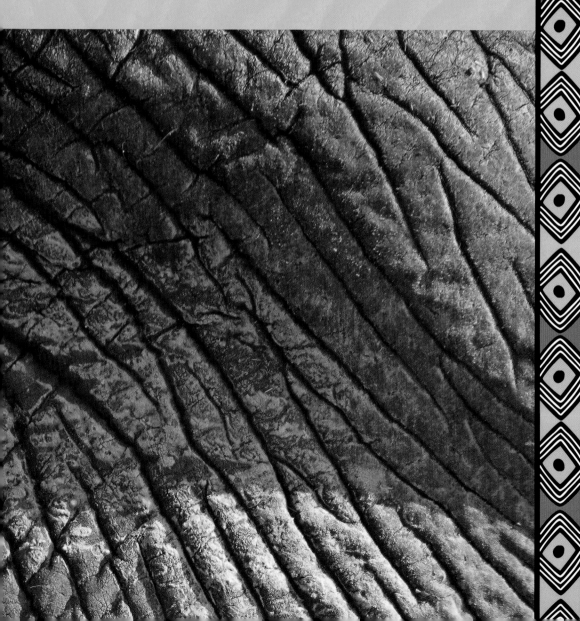

Elephants may be big, but they're remarkably delicate in many ways, says Caitlin. "Their wrinkly skin, for example, looks tough and impenetrable, but it's really sensitive." To protect it from sunburns and insect bites, elephants spray themselves with water, roll in the mud, and dust their bodies with dirt. "The wrinkles help them stay cool," notes Caitlin. When an elephant gets wet, water fills all its crinkly crevices, and the skin remains moist longer.

Elephants are believed to be smarter than most mammals and to have longer-term memories, says Caitlin. Brain-size comparisons between large mammals show that elephants have an extra-large temporal lobe—the area where sound cues are processed and within which is the hippocampus, where mammals form and store memories. This larger temporal lobe probably explains why more experienced matriarchs, who typically lead family groups, can readily distinguish the vocalizations of friends versus foes and recall where to find food and water during a drought.

Perhaps most striking—and the characteristic that intrigued Caitlin most early on—

The wrinkles in an elephant's skin help keep it cool. While it may look thick and tough, elephant skin is actually very sensitive—especially to insect bites.

is that elephants are highly social animals that form life-long relationships. They often engage in ritualistic behaviors that seem to mark special events. When a baby is born, or when they're reunited with old friends, elephants will trumpet, scream, and roar wildly. "They'll also use body language," says Caitlin, who has since witnessed many such joyous occasions in her career. "They'll flap their ears and embrace with their trunks," she says. "Strangely, they'll also pee and poop as part of the celebration."

As elephants travel across vast tracts of land, families frequently send vocal messages and coordinate their movements until they meet again. When a family member dies along the way, elephants become extremely curious about the remains. They've been observed lingering around a body for days, touching it with their feet, stroking it with their trunk, and even sometimes covering it with clumps of grass and other bits of earth. They're also curious about the skulls and bones of unrelated elephants and will often examine their remains extensively with their trunk and feet—even after the animal has been dead for some time.

The more Caitlin learned about elephants, their relationships, and their strong bonds, the more intrigued she was with their world—and the stronger her desire to protect them. Now it was time to work with the farmers of the Caprivi and explore the elephants' intricate behaviors and communications more closely in the field.

An elephant matriarch's long-term memory helps her distinguish the vocalizations of friends from those of unfamiliar elephants. It also enables her to remember migration paths and places to eat during droughts.

SCIENCE ON THE SAVANNAH

Caitlin and Tim arrived in the Caprivi during the rainy season, which runs from about December to April. In these Namibian summer months, violent thunderstorms soak the sun-parched land and new life abounds—insects swarm the skies, newborn elephants scamper by their mother, and plants flourish in the replenished soils.

After Caitlin settled into the area, she prepared for her new job by meeting with local leaders to learn more about the region, its people, and their relationship with the elephants. Not surprisingly, some villagers were suspicious of her as an outsider, but others recognized that she had come to help protect their crops. When harvest time rolled around in

Caitlin and a ranger colleague visit a farm the day after an elephant ate most of the year's supply of corn.

May, the sweet smell of corn filled the air and the threat of elephant raids loomed large. It was only a matter of time before the huge animals would invite themselves to dinner, and farmers would try everything they could to scare them away—from banging drums and lighting night fires to sleeping in the fields and firing warning gunshots.

Sure enough, the elephants struck again, and Caitlin witnessed the damage firsthand. Authorities took her to a cornfield trampled by a group of seven elephant bulls that had been raiding crops along the nearby Kwando River for several seasons. Caitlin and her guides followed the path of broken cornstalks. The elephant tracks started inside the reserve and cut across the river and into the field.

Caitlin measured the length of the elephants' hind footprints, which were "perfectly cast in the soft sand." This would help her approximate the ages of the animals. "The length of the back foot is correlated with an elephant's shoulder height," says Caitlin, who learned this from reading the research of other scientists. "Shoulder height scales with the number and wear of molars in an elephant's jaw. Together, the measurements give us an estimate of age." One footprint she measured belonged to an elephant calculated to be in the prime of his life at about forty years old.

"Elephant footprints are similar to human thumbprints," explains Caitlin. "The wrinkles and cracks on the bottom of the foot make a pattern in the sand that's similar to an ink print of a thumb." An elephant can give away its identity by the pattern of cracks and wearing of the sole of

An elephant's age can be estimated by the length of its hind foot. Here Caitlin measures the footprint of an elephant after he leaves the area, while her research assistant, Kaatri Nambandi, notes the measurement in a log.

FACING PAGE: Elephant footprints are similar to human thumbprints. Some elephants have distinct patterns that make them easy to identify. Note the bald patch at the heel.

RIGHT: Caitlin and village community game guards work with farmers to build electrical fences so that elephants will stay away from people's crops.

the foot—similar to the wearing of shoes. "This comes in handy when you're trying to identify individuals," she says. "Some elephants have distinct grooves or notches in their feet that give them away. Others leave prints that reveal a limp or indicate possible injuries."

After examining the elephants' footprints, Caitlin measured the farmer's cornfield using satellite navigation data from a global positioning system (GPS). The measurement helped her determine the amount of wire she'd need to build an electric fence around the crops. Caitlin decided, at least for the moment, that a jolt of electricity from a fence around the farmer's field would be the best—and quickest—way to keep both the crops and the elephants safe.

During that year and the two that followed, Caitlin built many electric fences with villagers. Slowly she gained the trust of the farmers and captured the intrigue of the local women. They marveled as the scientist mounted fences using "men's" tools, such as hammers, and called her "the mother of all elephants." To them, she cared so much about the elephants, it only made sense that she was their mother.

Caitlin also knew of deterrents that others had tried, including digging deep trenches around the fields and creating barriers with crops that the elephants didn't like to eat, such as red chilies. But these methods were difficult to implement. Instead she tried alarms using car sirens that were run off motorcycle batteries and triggered by a trip switch when the elephants entered a field. This method was inexpensive for farmers and easy to implement.

Still, she hoped to find a simpler, more natural way to discourage the elephants from the area.

THE HERDS AT ETOSHA

After the hectic harvest seasons in the Caprivi, Caitlin and Tim spent their summers (June and July) at Etosha National Park, where they continued their work. Life was slower at Etosha, with no farmer-elephant conflicts to address, and the peaceful environment allowed the scientists to calmly watch the elephants' behaviors unfold.

Caitlin especially enjoyed watching elephant families interact at the waterhole, where they'd gather during the hot, dry days. "Most elephants grow up with a mother and a grandmother, a few aunts, a couple of sisters, a brother or two, and lots of cousins as playmates," she says. "The youngsters generally have a ball together, dusting, sparring, rolling in the mud, and cavorting in the water. Older sisters typically care for the little ones when they're in trouble. I've seen them comfort their siblings after the babies have been stuck in the mud or teased by a bully."

Elephant families are hierarchical,

A baby elephant is quickly welcomed into a family's network of youngsters and forms strong bonds with siblings and cousins. Females live together for life, and males live in the family until they're about twelve to fifteen.

Matriarchs are always on the lookout for potential danger.

says Caitlin. "The wise matriarch leads the group and makes all the decisions about where to go and when. She determines when it's safe to approach a waterhole and when it's time to move on. The rest of the family follows her lead."

Male and female elephants also live in separate social groups most of their lives, meeting occasionally when they drink at rivers or water-holes and interacting during mating periods. "As a young bull grows into his teen years, his hormones surge and he turns feisty," says Caitlin. "He'll constantly test boundaries with his mother and sisters and begin to chase other animals. When the animals run away, the bull's confidence soars and he becomes even more of a menace. Over time, the bull gets fresh with his sisters and aunts, or even unfamiliar females from an unrelated group, to the point at which his mother has to give him a good jab with her tusk. This inevitably sends him bellowing off to safer territory. Soon, however, he's back to stir up trouble." Eventually, either the family pushes him out or he decides it's time to leave and he must learn to survive on his own in the bull world. Members of bull groups often follow the lead of more dominant males, who appear to keep the young members of the group in line. These dominant bulls seem to play an important role in providing structure, stability, and security in a younger bull's life.

25

ABOVE & LEFT: Adult females in a family group eventually become frustrated with the antics of young bulls that are coming of age and often will chase them aggressively. Here the female elephant demonstrates the seriousness of her intent by tusking the bull in the behind. Since young bulls are sometimes reluctant to leave their families, or stir up trouble in unrelated families, it will probably take many more "nudges" to persuade him to head out on his own.

FACING PAGE: When an adolescent bull spends more and more time away from his family, he may join a bull group that offers added protection and stability. Here an adult bull tends to an adolescent.

Studies show that when teenage bulls live in areas without older bulls, they prematurely go into a physiological state called musth (pronounced "must"). When a bull elephant is in musth, he produces a large amount of the male hormone testosterone, which makes him aggressive and motivated to find mates. This rush of testosterone can cause bulls to behave violently toward people and animals, as has been reported in parts of India, Asia, and Africa.

"With younger bulls, these violent episodes can be very erratic," says Caitlin.

In two South African reserves, for example, adolescent bulls that had been reintroduced to the parks had attacked and killed dozens of rhinos. After investigating, park managers guessed that one of the problems might be that the young bulls were suffering from too much testosterone in their system, and they brought in some larger, older elephants to take control of the situation. As anticipated, the presence of the mature bulls ultimately suppressed the teenage bulls' hormones and helped calm their unruly behaviors.

FANCY FOOTWORK

It was during Caitlin's visits to Etosha that she first noticed the elephants "freezing" like planthoppers when listening for the arrival of other herds. When she saw the huge mammals stopping in their tracks and leaning forward on their front feet, she began to wonder if vibrations in the ground could hold important messages for elephants.

An elephant's foot has a fatty heel.

"An elephant walks on its tiptoes, with its weight forward," she explains. "Supporting each foot—and the weight of the elephant—is a cushiony pad of dense fat at the heel. I wondered whether that cushion served more than one practical purpose." Caitlin knew that the pads in an elephant's foot contained a rich oil that people once used to harvest for their oil lamps. As she and her colleagues investigated further, using samples from a dead elephant, she found that the dense fat was similar to what other researchers call "acoustic fat" (sound-associated fat) in marine mammals. Acoustic fat helps animals such as dolphins send and receive sound vibrations in the water. This led Caitlin to think that acoustic-like fat in the elephant's foot may help with the transmission of low-frequency signals to and from the ground via the fatty footpad.

30

"Perhaps the elephants were listening to sounds that traveled from their feet and toes to their ears," Caitlin

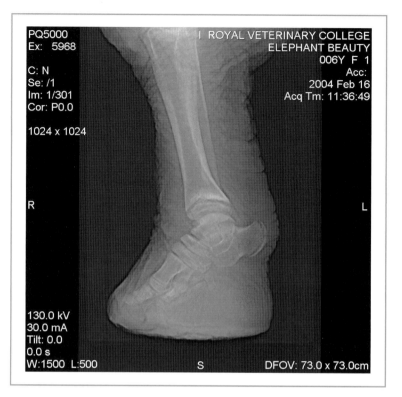

ABOVE: As this computerized tomography (CT) scan shows, the elephant stands on its tiptoes and rests on a cushiony pad at the heel.

LEFT: Caitlin monitors the elephants from her field recording station. The scientist first began recording elephant calls at Mushara to see if she could find an alarm call that could be used as an effective tool to keep the animals away from farmers' fields.

An elephant family group flees in response to one of Caitlin's recorded alarm calls.

surmised. "These low-level vibrations in the ground might be byproducts of the elephants' booming voices and footfalls, which were so forceful they shook the earth. As a result, their greetings, mating calls, and alarm signals might not only travel through the air as sound waves, but might also ripple through the ground."

Caitlin grew excited about the possibilities. To begin testing her theory, she recorded various elephant calls while at Etosha. She not only wanted to know how the elephants communicated, but also hoped to identify an alarm call that would be an effective tool in keeping elephants away from farmers' fields. Up until then, she had been using loud noises such as car alarms to scare away the animals, but she knew it would be only a matter of time before they realized no real danger existed. "I figured that in the long run the elephants' own alarms would be the most meaningful to them," she says.

At first, the elephant calls that Caitlin recorded all sounded the same to her. But after a while, she noticed subtle differences. Angry and excited calls, for example, varied more in pitch—from low to high and back to low again. "Let's go" calls—which a leader used to summon a group to get moving—were flatter in tone.

During one of her trips to Mushara waterhole, Caitlin recorded several alarm calls that a group of elephants had made to alert others about lions in the area. "The calls had a steep rise in pitch in the middle, much steeper than other calls I had recorded," she says. Caitlin made a special tape of these alarm calls and played it back on a boom box to different elephant herds in three regions of the park to see how they'd respond. "I'd wait until the elephants had a chance to drink before playing the calls," she says, "and I videotaped each trial." The researcher also noted the size and ages of the elephants in the group, along with any distinguishing features.

At Mushara waterhole, the response to the recorded alarm calls was immediate. "The elephants ran off with their heads up and tails pointing straight behind them," says Caitlin, who played the tape to six different family groups.

The intense reactions surprised Caitlin. Clearly she was on to something. Still, she decided to limit the number of experimental trials to as few as possible so as not to needlessly stress the elephants. She then reviewed the videotapes over and over to determine which calls produced the strongest responses. After identifying three deep rumbles in particular, she created a new tape and played it to the elephants.

The instant fear responses at Mushara told the scientist that these were the three rumbles that mattered. When she played the tape at two other sites in Etosha, however, the reactions were less dramatic. "It was as if they didn't think the alarm calls were directed at them," says Caitlin. "Some of the elephants even became aggressive and behaved as if they wanted to fight the 'caller,' which in this case was me and my hidden boom box."

Why did some elephants react fearfully to the alarm calls, while others became angry? Was there one alarm that all elephants would respond to in the same way? And how were the elephants receiving these messages? Were they listening to the calls with their ears and their feet? "I was filled with questions after the initial experiments," says Caitlin.

An elephant matriarch gives Caitlin an aggressive head shake in response to an alarm call playback.

SCHOOL DAYS

A geophone measures vibrations traveling in the earth. These instruments are used by geophysicists to measure the movement of the earth during earthquakes, for example.

When the dry season ended, Caitlin and Tim returned to the Caprivi to work with villagers. The pair continued to study elephants in Namibia for three years before returning to the United States to resume their education. "It was difficult to leave," says Caitlin. "I had come to love the people, the elephants, and the land, but I knew there was still much to learn before I could really be of help to them."

While attending the University of California, Davis, Caitlin continued her research as part of her doctoral studies in ecology—the study of organisms and how they interact with each other and the environment. "I wanted to explore my theory that elephants communicate through ground vibrations," she says. "And if they did, I still hoped to apply what I learned from this novel communication pathway to better understand elephants and perhaps help manage them more effectively."

Caitlin began building a case for her seismic communication theory one experiment at a time. Her first challenge was to prove that elephants generate vibrations in the ground with their rumbles and footfalls. With the help of two scientists, including Lynette Hart, her Ph.D. advisor, and Byron Arnason, a geophysicist—an expert in measuring the movements of the earth—she was able to do just that. The researchers set up their vibration measuring equipment at an elephant facility in Texas, where they buried a series of geophones in the ground and strategically placed microphones nearby.

Then they waited for the elephants to talk.

"At one point, the keeper sparked the 'conversation' by playing the elephant's favorite game: 'chase the chicken out of the enclosure,'" says Caitlin. "The elephants were so thrilled by the game, they gleefully blasted out rumbles and charged around the yard." From this, the team captured the necessary acoustic and seismic recordings to support their theory. Using a recording system to capture acoustic signals and a separate system to capture vibrations in the ground, the researchers were able to show that the same sounds recorded in two different environments were behaving differently. "This meant that the ground signals had a velocity [speed or rate of propagation] of their own and were not simply airborne sound waves bouncing in and out of the ground, traveling at the same rate. When the results turned out to be what we had hoped, we were tempted to trumpet and roar ourselves. Now we could proceed knowing that the vibrations traveling in the ground were indeed a separate signal with its own velocity and integrity."

Soon after the success of this and other experiments, Caitlin and her colleagues published a paper with their findings and gained worldwide attention from scientists and reporters alike. As interest in her work grew, the scientist began receiving research grants to return to Mushara waterhole, this time to determine whether elephants were able to detect vibrational ground signals as well as to produce them—that is, were they really able to "listen

through their limbs" as Caitlin had suspected?

"I was eager to go back to the wild and test my hypothesis," says Caitlin. "Only this time I'd have a research team to help, as well as sophisticated measuring equipment and a twenty-foot observation tower where we could watch the elephants come and go." The return trip would be the first of Caitlin's many visits back to Namibia.

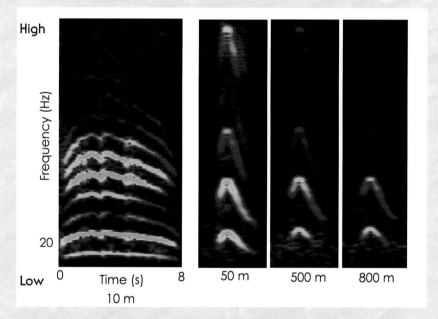

These spectrograms are visual representations of sound. They illustrate one elephant's calls or vocalizations as they travel through the air. The graphic on the left shows the sound waves generated from an eight-second vocalization that was recorded ten meters away from the elephant. These low frequency calls are emitted in the range of 10–20 Hz, below human hearing. The graphic on the right shows the sound waves recorded by microphones that were 50, 500, and 800 meters from the elephant. Notice how the low-frequency components of the sound waves (bottom two) travel greater distances than the high-frequency components.

SETTLING INTO CAMP

As in earlier years, Caitlin visited the Mushara site in June and July. During these dry months, water supplies dwindle in other areas of the park and the elephants regularly return to the waterhole to drink. These routine visits by the animals allow Caitlin and her team to watch the elephants interact and note their social relationships. "Pecking orders exist within elephant families, as well as between them," Caitlin says, "and it's interesting to watch the groups jockey for the best position at the waterhole. It doesn't take long to see who sits at the top of the family hierarchy."

Caitlin chose Mushara for her experiments because many elephants visit this site and because the alarm calls she planned to play back had originally been recorded there. "Since the elephants responded immediately to the calls when I played them through the air, I thought that they might also react when I played them through the ground."

In the dry season, many animals congregate at Mushara waterhole. On an extremely hot day, elephants can clear the area of other species to make room for a large family group.

Setting up camp involves several days of work, which is followed by a few more for the installation of research equipment.

Soon after Caitlin and her team arrived at the field site, they set up a screen of boma cloth—a tan material that animals can't see through and which they perceive as a solid object. "The boma cloth hid our movements and activities throughout the field season so that we weren't disturbing the animals," she says. "Giraffes in particular have keen eyesight, and any unusual movement can cause them to wait at the edge of the clearing for hours before deeming it safe to approach the water—sometimes for very good reason."

Once the boma cloth was in place, the researchers set up an electric fence around it for added security against

Giraffes have keen eyesight, in part so they can keep tabs on one another while foraging in tall trees.

An adult male lion is always on the lookout for distracted animals at the waterhole. Note the boma cloth in the distance around the research tower that helps hide the activities of the team.

curious lions. They then dug a long-drop outhouse and assembled their kitchen tent, tables, mess kits, coolers, cast-iron pots, and everything else needed to cook their meals. "This included two hundred pounds of butternut squash, which is the best staple food in a place with little refrigeration," says Caitlin.

Next they assembled a solar-energy charging system with two eighty-watt solar panels and six car batteries—a pair of batteries for each floor of the tower, as well as for the kitchen and lab on the ground. "The solar-energy system charged our computers, video cameras, tape recorder, and

camera batteries," says Caitlin. "It also powered the elephant-dung dryer that dries dung samples for later hormone analysis in a lab, and a small twelve-volt refrigerator where dairy products and cold drinks are stored."

At the end of the day, team members pitched their tents and unpacked their belongings. "It was a relief to complete much of the hard work and to begin making our own little cozy homes for the next two months," says Caitlin. "Now we were ready to set up the seismic equipment and begin tracking the elephants."

41

FACING PAGE: Fully operational, the Mushara tower and research camp houses about eight people. It includes a kitchen, dining area, tents, outhouse, and solar charging station, as well as a dung research station.

LEFT: Some elephant bulls are curious about the researchers' camp as well as the electric fence. This bull inspects it before it's turned on for the night.

EARS TO THE GROUND

Tim Rodwell buries shakers—used as low-frequency vibration transmitters—next to the waterhole to play back elephant vocalizations through the ground.

For the first three weeks, Caitlin and her team collected information about the elephants and prepared for their much-anticipated experiments. "We started by burying shakers—the same devices that shake your house in a home theater to provide a more sensory movie experience," says Caitlin. "We planted the shakers near the waterhole and used them to play back the low-frequency elephant vibrations through the ground."

The researchers also placed a geophone near each shaker. Geophones record the vibration levels of elephant calls in the ground much like a microphone records vibrations in the air. They are also used to ensure that the playback recordings are at levels representative of an actual elephant signal. The team placed a microphone near the shakers so they would be alerted if the vibrations were played so loudly that they could be heard in the air. "We did this to make sure the elephants were only responding to the earth's vibrations," she says.

During the experiments, Caitlin and her team monitored the elephants before, during, and after transmitting the ground vibrations and looked for behaviors indicating that the animals were paying attention. "We scored behaviors such as freezing, scanning back and forth in the air with their ears held out,

orienting toward the source of the vibrations, and bunching into tighter groups," says Caitlin. "Bunching behavior occurs when older females sense danger and gather their little ones underneath them. One minute the elephants could be spread out across the pan, and the next minute they would be bunched into small family groups—young ones in the center and the adult females fanning out to face the threat."

Finally, her moment of discovery came, after several failed attempts because of faulty equipment and too many elephants at the waterhole.

I was on watch in the tower until two-thirty in the morning on a frigid cold night—waiting and waiting for elephants to arrive. Periodically, I'd shift in my chair and scan the horizon using a night vision monocular. At about eleven o'clock, I heard a soft rumble and saw a herd at the edge of the clearing. At last, I thought, my first subjects of the night. I turned on my walkie-talkie and woke up the team so that they could prepare for our experiment.

As the elephants reached the waterhole, we documented their arrival time and counted each one. Then we waited several minutes for the group to settle down and drink. When enough time had passed, we started a control period within which time we monitored the animals' normal behaviors. Then we played back the alarm call that I had recorded years earlier to see how and if they'd respond. I whispered, "Start," and the team delivered the seismic signal once every minute for three minutes. After that, we observed and collected data on the elephants' reactions for the next five minutes.

I watched the elephants in awe. They didn't respond by running away, as they had in the acoustic trials. Their responses were subtler and dramatic in a different way. The whole group suddenly froze in unison—some of them dropping the water in their trunks mid-drink. Those that were walking to reposition themselves at the waterhole froze midstride, with some shifting their weight and leaning forward. The place was absolutely silent.

Then slowly, almost imperceptibly, many of the elephants turned toward the source of the signal—a shaker buried nearby. Within a minute or so, each family bunched into its individual units in a defensive posture, with the little ones in the center. I couldn't believe my eyes. The entire herd had responded—just as I had witnessed years ago.

My heart pounded. We had finally demonstrated that my original hunch was true: Elephants can sense and respond to seismic cues.

Caitlin tried to quiet her excitement. She still had to prove statistically—with the numbers—that the pattern of response was consistent with many elephant groups. And, in time, that's exactly what she did. After multiple experiments with different families, she and the team collected enough scientific evidence to report that elephants do indeed talk to each other through the ground.

"Our results show that elephants can detect and respond appropriately to vibrations in the ground caused by other elephants' low-frequency vocalizations—sounds below the range of human hearing," says Caitlin. These seismic signals may help ensure the elephants' long-term survival by giving them another communications channel to coordinate their movements over long distances, send messages to potential mates, and broadcast warnings about impending danger.

Elephants approach the waterhole at sunset.

Using low-light binoculars, Caitlin and her team watch the elephants approach the waterhole at sunset. They record their subjects' behaviors in an electronic data logger.

With night vision equipment (light-intensifying gear) attached to the video recorder, the team can observe the elephants' interactions at the waterhole in the dark.

DONNA THE SCHOLAR

Once Caitlin established that elephants sent messages to each other through the ground, she shared her discovery with the world in scientific articles and eventually in a book called *The Elephant's Secret Sense*. Next she wanted to know: How far and powerfully do these signals travel? To find out, she enlisted the help of a 9,000-pound African elephant named Donna at the Oakland Zoo in California.

"Ecologists try to have a field environment, where they can observe behaviors in the wild, as well as a controlled environment, where they can manipulate those behaviors and test their true meaning," says Caitlin. By working with an elephant that's easily trained, such as Donna, Caitlin can test the sensitivity of the elephant's feet in terms of how far away it might be able to detect another elephant communicating. "It's sort of like giving her a hearing test for the feet," she says.

Caitlin teamed with Colleen Kinzley, the general curator at the Oakland

The trainer Colleen Kinzley gives Donna, an elephant at the Oakland Zoo, a treat.

Zoo, and they began working closely with Donna. First they trained their eager student to lift her foot when she heard an elephant rumble. Then they taught her to lift her foot when she *felt* a rumble vibrating in the ground through a shaker. Finally, they taught Donna to respond with her trunk instead of her foot, so that she could use all four of her feet to concentrate on the seismic vibrations.

During the experiments, Donna stands on a big metal plate a few feet away from Caitlin and rests her trunk on a starting post until the trial begins. Colleen, the trainer, faces Donna so she doesn't know whether or not a signal will be delivered. This keeps her from accidentally influencing the elephant's choices. "Ready," says Caitlin. "Go ahead," replies Colleen to the scientist, who then either triggers a low-level vibration through cables in the ground or does nothing and waits for Donna's reaction. When Donna feels a vibration, she touches a square target that means "yes" with her trunk. When she doesn't feel a vibration, she touches a triangular target that means "no" with her trunk. Each correct answer wins Donna plenty of "Good girl!" calls from Colleen and a food treat, such as an alfalfa cube, bread, or an apple wafer (horse cookie). This makes Donna give off a noise that's similar to a cat purring, called a raspberry.

Missing, however, often upsets her. "When we started to reduce the ground vibration levels lower and lower to see how well Donna could sense them, she began to fail more often, and became frustrated," says Caitlin. In one series of tests, she became so disappointed that she threw the target poles at the researchers.

To date, Caitlin continues to test for the lowest vibration level that Donna can detect—called an absolute threshold—and she's getting closer. "Donna's probably not as sensitive as an elephant that grew up in the wild, where vibration detection is much more important for survival than in a zoo," explains Caitlin. "But her test results give us a good indication of the possible ranges. Our best estimate of potential detection is in the range of two to four kilometers, but under ideal conditions, may be on the order of tens of kilometers."

47

When female elephants sense danger, they often gather their young ones underneath them and fan out to face the threat. This behavior is called bunching, and Caitlin repeatedly saw it after transmitting the seismic alarm call in her experiments. When elephants bunch, it indicates that they're being vigilant or wary.

During a memory test, Donna the elephant touches a photograph of a banana after being shown a real banana.

Hearing tests aren't the only way Donna the elephant is advancing science. She's also helping Caitlin learn more about elephant memories. Long-term memory is especially critical to elephants because they need to remember important things such as where to find food during times of drought.

"In this study, we're trying to show that elephants—like several other intelligent social animals—can represent objects in their mind," says Caitlin. "So, for example, we'll present a real banana to Donna and then later ask her to pick out a banana from three pictures: one of a banana, one of an apple, and one of an orange." When an animal can recognize and represent an object in its mind, it's the first step toward demonstrating that it also can imagine that object in a different time and place—such as an elephant imagin-ing and remembering the time and place when a particular fruit tree has ripe fruit to eat. "This differs from a dog remembering where a bone had once been buried," says Caitlin, "because the dog's memory is based on a perceptual cue—smelling the bone and remembering the smell of it—instead of a representation (a photograph) with no olfactory cue."

CALLER IDs

As Caitlin continued to visit Mushara each year to study elephant communication in the wild, she made more and more amazing discoveries. Not only can elephants detect ground vibrations, she learned, but they can also discriminate subtle differences between these vibrations through their feet. That is, they can tell whether calls in the wild come from trusted friends—such as other family members—or from strangers.

An elephant sometimes rolls a front foot forward and presses its toenails into the ground, presumably to detect vibrations by way of bone conduction.

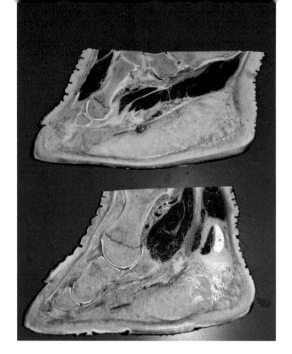

Pictured above right is the bottom of an elephant's foot. Caitlin and her team dissected a foot (slices on the left) to find the vibration-sensitive cells called Pacinian corpuscles. These are the cells that look like onions, as the bottom right picture shows.

The scientist followed her field experiments with anatomical studies (those involving the physical body) and teamed with the Stanford veterinary pathologist Donna Bouley and the student Christine Alarcon to investigate the vibration-sensitive cells in an elephant's foot. She started by identifying special cells called Pacinian corpuscles (KOR-pus-ils) and then counting how many were present across the bottom of the foot. "Pacinian corpuscles are cells that look like onions and have many nested layers that shift in response to a vibration," says Caitlin. "The shifting layers of cells cause a nerve impulse to be sent to the brain," she explains.

One way elephants detect vibrations rippling across the surface of the earth is through these vibration-sensitive cells in their feet and trunk, says Caitlin. "The special cells allow the animals to feel the tiniest of movements." This is especially true in the trunk tip, which researchers have found to have an extraordinary

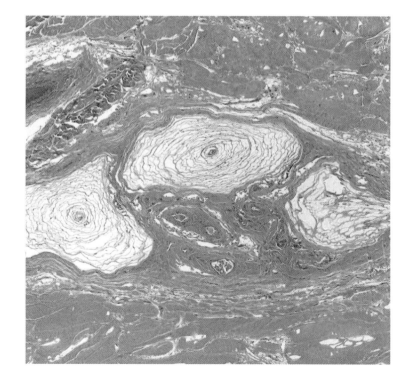

Elephants have many vibration-sensitive cells in the tip of their trunk. This allows them to feel the smallest of movements in the ground.

concentration of these cells. After her own investigations, Caitlin determined that the trunk was probably more sensitive to vibrations than the foot. "This would explain why dominant individuals in both family and bull groups spend a lot of time with their trunks on the ground before choosing which way to go," says Caitlin. "By presumably using the trunk to determine the safest direction for travel, it would minimize potentially negative encounters, such as unfriendly animals or people in trucks."

Another way elephants detect vibrations is through a pathway from the toe bones to their middle ears. "With bone conduction, the toes of the listening elephant pick up the vibrations, which travel up the legs and into the skull and middle ear," explains Caitlin. "These vibrations shake the middle ear bones—just as an airborne sound would—and the message is sent to the inner ear and on to the brain. Humans can also hear sounds through bone conduction," she says. "The easiest way to experience this is to place your fingers in your ears and listen to your voice being amplified by your skull."

Since the elephants demonstrated that they could recognize callers through the ground, Caitlin began to question whether recorded alarm calls would successfully keep family groups away from farmers' cornfields. "I needed to find a call that would work with a wide range of elephants—regardless of who made the call," she says. "This made me think about male elephants and their interest in estrus females—cows that are ready to mate and repeatedly make long calls, apparently to advertise their hormonal state. Perhaps male elephants looking for mates would be less discriminating than normal, and I could use calls made by these females as a tool to 'attract' problem bulls away from farms."

After a series of experiments using playbacks of estrus calls to adult, teen, and young adult bull elephants, Caitlin found that all bulls—except one small group of adults that were not in musth—displayed interest. "Interested bulls turned from their departure paths and walked in the direction of the playback calls each time they detected the signal," she says. Given the success of the studies, Caitlin wants to work with park officials in Namibia to peacefully attract bulls back to their "homes" within protected areas when they stray. "This would be much more preferable to some of the current aggressive measures," she says, such as firing gunshots in the air, corralling the elephants with vehicles, or in some cases outright killing them.

51

A dominant elephant bull (center) and his peers and subordinates head to the Mushara waterhole.

long line of bull elephants appears on the horizon. The dominant animal holds his head high as the others swing their giant heads back and forth to the beat of their gait. Left feet forward, then right—left and right, moving one side forward and then the other, as if they have left and right skis attached to their front and back feet. "This unique gait—or walk cycle—is one reason elephants seem to float as they walk," says Caitlin, who has traveled to Mushara on yet another mission.

Her new goal? To study bull elephant behavior and male social structure—an area few scientists have had the opportunity to observe and document, but which Caitlin has been privy to in her communications studies. "I want to learn more about the bulls' social network," she says. "Who befriends whom? Who are the dominant individuals and how long can they hold their position? Whom do the females prefer? And who is low-ranking and why? Much has been learned about dominance in matriarchal family groups and their extended social networks," she says. "I want to understand the structure of bull relationships." Caitlin hopes that the knowledge she gains from studying male elephant societies will bring a deeper understanding of other male groups, including those of humans.

During her visits to Etosha, the scientist and her team are measuring bull interactions to determine who behaves in a friendly way most often and who is more likely to be aggressive and under what conditions. The researchers have compiled an elephant behavior catalog—called an ethogram—in which they score each bull behavior as it happens. These include *affiliative,* or bonding, behaviors, such as gentle sparring, touching, and pushing; *comfort* behaviors, such as drinking, bathing, and resting; and *aggressive* behaviors, such as charging, chasing, and head-shaking.

An ear fold is an aggressive posture in which an elephant holds its ears out and folds them. This pushes the lower part of the ear back and creates a raised crease in the middle.

Caitlin teaches her student, Mindi Summers, how to use the bull identification book, which contains drawings and pictures of an elephant's key features.

Elephant bulls may engage in combat that can lead to mortal injuries.

FACING PAGE: Two bull elephants share a moment of mutual affection by wrapping their trunks and leaning their heads toward each other.

RIGHT: The elephant named Greg has two large tabs and a small tab missing from the middle of his left ear. He was named Greg after the head elephant keeper at the Oakland Zoo when Caitlin first set up her bull study.

57

"Bull elephant behavior is fascinating," says Caitlin. "It's almost haunting how their social dynamics mirror ours in the way they form all-male groups—similar to fraternities—and engage in ritualized fighting, similar to wrestling matches." Caitlin is also finding that most animals live up to their reputation. "One bull we've nicknamed Kevin is a bully who likes to spar with everyone, while Willie Nelson is a raggedy but gentle and well-respected elephant."

Why the colorful names? "They help us remember individuals and are linked to physical attributes," says Caitlin. Captain Picard, for example, has a bald tail, and Billy Idol has multiple ear piercings. Along with the names, each bull

receives a catalog number that the researchers log in an identification book.

"The identification book includes drawings and pictures of each elephant's key features," explains Caitlin. "We keep track of ear notches, tusk shape, tail hair, and overall size of the bulls to distinguish one from another. The features combine to form a bull 'fingerprint' so that we can identify individuals using natural traits instead of having to tag or mark them. Some of the toughest bulls to identify are new young bulls, because their ears show less wear and tear than the older ones."

Smokey has a large, shallow crescent-shaped cutout in the middle of his right ear, along with a few small divots and holes.

Tim has a crescent-shaped cutout in the middle of his left ear, which has a tab dangling from the bottom and a hole next to the tab.

Greg's page in the Elephant ID book highlights his broken tusks, sparse tail hair, and tears on his left ear.

During the final sunset of the season, Caitlin watches Big Momma and her family drinking at the waterhole. One of the bulls that Caitlin is studying comes from Big Momma's family group.

SEASON'S END

As the sun sets and the bulls exit the waterhole, Caitlin sneaks in a few last photos. It's the end of another field season, and the following day is a big one. "Packing camp is never easy," she says. "There's lots of work, and things have to be done in order so that we remain safe while we break down our security perimeter and pack up our equipment."

The next morning, the team dines on a hearty breakfast of corn porridge (a local staple) with raisins, nuts, honey, and butter and begins the final breakdown. "One group takes down the shower, and another buries the hole for the toilet. Then we dismantle the kitchen and the dung-processing station and pack all the recording equipment. Finally, we bundle up the tents and personal belongings, such as hats, coats, and sweaters."

By the end of the day, the truck's piled high with paraphernalia. "We eat a quick dinner of vegetable curry and admire the elephants one last night," says Caitlin. "At dawn, we roll out of bed and pack the last few items: our sleeping bags, our bedrolls, and ourselves.

"Until next year . . ."

Getting everything to fit back in the truck at the end of a season is a challenge. But fortunately, Caitlin's local colleague from the Etosha Ecological Institute, Johannes Kapner, is there to provide a helping hand.

ELEPHANTS IN PERIL

Elephants once roamed the earth in great numbers, from Africa to China. Today, world wildlife officials estimate the Asian elephant population at an endangered 20,000 and the overall African elephant population at a "vulnerable" 500,000—down from as many as 10 million African and Asian elephants a hundred years ago.

Major threats to the animals include poaching—the illegal killing of elephants for their ivory tusks and other body parts—and a loss of habitat. In Asia and Africa, for example, elephant habitats continue to shrink as people clear more forests to build farms and developments. Less land for the animals often means less food for them to eat.

Elephants in different regions experience different issues, says Caitlin. In some parts of South Africa, such as Kruger National Park, some managers believe that overpopulation is a problem. Too many elephants now live in the protected area, and they're putting other animals at risk as they deplete the land.

Poaching also remains a huge threat to African elephants—especially in central and east Africa. The elephant death rate from illegal hunting in these areas is higher than ever, reports biologist Samuel Wasser. What's different today is that most people don't realize the elephant's current plight, he says. Political instability in central Africa, for instance, has led to more guns in the area, and some people are using them to kill elephants for food as well as ivory.

Some scientists believe that along with physical threats elephants may be suffering from psychological stress caused by years of poaching, habitat loss, and culls—where elephant families have been killed to control populations. Elephants form deep relationships, note scientists, and calves that watch family members being shot and killed may be at high risk for depression and violent behaviors later in life.

Given the wide range of physical and mental stresses on wild elephants—revealed, in part, by their sudden rise in violent acts—Caitlin believes it's more important than ever to learn more about their natural behaviors to help protect them. For example, over time, Caitlin realized that there was a pattern of heightened aggression exhibited by younger elephants during wet years relative to dry years, when there didn't seem

Elephants hold their ears straight out and face a challenger squarely when angry, often with their head held up.

to be as much oversight by the older bulls because there were many places to drink besides Mushara. As such, the younger elephants did not have to spend as much time with their elders, and they were showing signs of going into musth earlier than they would have otherwise. This pattern reflects what was seen in the reserves in South Africa where young bulls were reintroduced without older bulls. Through her research into elephant communications, the dynamics of their social networks, and hormone expression patterns, the scientist hopes to help better understand what the animals need not only to survive but to thrive, so we can ensure their future as a species.

Caitlin and a research assistant, Christina Alarcon, collect a fresh dung sample from an elephant that's at the waterhole behind them. Once dried and sifted, the dung samples are taken back to a laboratory, where Caitlin's colleague Sam Wasser and his team determine hormone levels. The hormones testosterone and cortisol are assessed and then compared with aggressive and stressful interactions to see how well they match.

ADOPT AN ELEPHANT

If you want to help elephants, consider talking with your family about adopting one or more from organizations such as Defenders of Wildlife (www.defenders.org), which works to protect wild animals and their habitats. Elephant scientist Caitlin O'Connell and her husband, Tim Rodwell, also offer an elephant sponsorship program through their organization, called Utopia Scientific.

"The program fosters research and works to reduce conflict between elephants and farmers outside of Etosha National Park in Namibia," says Caitlin. "Sponsors get to know an elephant of their choice up close and personal, while contributing to elephant research and management." Along with a photo of their elephant, sponsors receive a detailed description of its physical features, approximate age, personality traits, friends and rivals, and ranking within its group. They also receive updates on any outstanding or peculiar behaviors observed by researchers during the field season. Proceeds from the program go to research, conservation, and monitoring of Etosha elephants.

To learn more about this program and discover other ways to help elephants, visit the Utopia Scientific site at www.utopiascientific.org.

Trunk-over-head is an affiliative, or bonding, behavior in which an older bull places his trunk up over a younger bull's head and rests his head there. This behavior is most likely to occur between bonded individuals and is a sign of affection from a higher-ranking bull to a lower-ranking one.

EXPLORATIONS

PUBLICATIONS

Elephant **(Eyewitness Books)** by Ian Redmond
   (Dorling Kindersley, 2000)

Elephants **(World Life Library)** by Joyce Poole
   (Voyageur Press, Inc., 1997)

The Elephant Book by Ian Redmond (Candlewick Press, 2003)

The Elephant Hospital by Kathy Darling, photographs by
   Tara Darling (Millbrook Press, 2002)

ADULT BOOKS BY CAITLIN O'CONNELL

An Elephant's Life (Lyons Press, 2011)

The Elephant's Secret Sense (Free Press, 2007;
   paperback by Chicago University Press, 2008)

DVDS

Echo of the Elephants (BBC Worldwide Ltd. Program, 2005)

Echo and Other Elephants: Enchanting Stories of an Elephant Family
   (BBC Worldwide Ltd. Program, 2008)

WEB LINKS

Amboseli Trust for Elephants: elephanttrust.org

ElephantVoices: elephantvoices.org

The David Sheldrick Wildlife Trust: sheldrickwildlifetrust.org

The Elephants of Africa: www.pbs.org/wnet/nature/elephants

Utopia Scientific: www.utopiascientific.org

World Wildlife Fund: www.worldwildlife.org/species/finder/
   africanelephants/item399.html

Watch Caitlin's elephant experiments!

Acoustic Alarm Call Playback Video:
www.utopiascientific.org/Videos/EleHerdScare.html

Seismic Alarm Call Playback Video:
www.utopiascientific.org/Videos/SeisWarn21.html

Estrus Call Playback Video:
www.utopiascientific.org/Videos/Ele108.html

PACHYDERM TERMS

AFRICAN ELEPHANT: the largest living land animal in the world.

ALPHA MALE: a lead bull elephant.

ASIAN ELEPHANT: a smaller distant relative of the African elephant that has round ears and a dome-shaped back. They live in places such as India and Southeast Asia and are highly endangered.

BOMA CLOTH: a tan material that animals can't see through and that's used as a screen to keep animals from entering observation areas.

BULL: a male elephant.

BULL IDENTIFICATION BOOK: a log of drawings and pictures with characteristic features of each male elephant, such as ear notches and tusk shape.

BUNCHING: a behavior that occurs when older female elephants sense danger and gather young ones underneath them and fan out to face the threat.

CALF: a baby elephant.

CAPRIVI: an area in northeastern Namibia where Caitlin worked to reduce conflict over resources between villagers and elephants.

CONSERVATIONIST: a person who works to protect the environment and animal species.

COW: a female elephant.

DNA: the chemical blueprint that makes people and animals who and what they are.

ECOLOGY: the study of organisms and their relationships to one another and the environment.

ELECTRIC FENCE: a barrier that releases a jolt of electricity when animals touch it. It's one method villagers use to keep elephants away from their crops.

ELEPHANT BEHAVIOR CATALOG (ETHOGRAM): a list of the different types of elephant behaviors used in research.

ESTRUS FEMALES: elephant cows that are ready to mate.

ETOSHA NATIONAL PARK: a reserve in Namibia, Africa, that spans 13,838 square miles and is home to a variety of animals.

FAMILY GROUP: a group of female elephants, usually including the matriarch, her sisters, daughters, and nieces, and their offspring.

FIELD BIOLOGIST: a person who studies nature and living organisms in their natural environments.

GAIT: an elephant's walking pattern.

GENETICS: the study of heredity and how genes affect behaviors.

GEOPHONE: a magnet and coil tool scientists use to measure vibrations traveling in the earth.

HERD: a large group of animals, such as elephants.

HORMONES: chemicals released in the body that affect it in numerous ways.

MATRIARCH: the female head of the family group.

MIGRATE: to move from one place to another.

MUSHARA: a waterhole at the eastern corner of Etosha National Park where the elephant scientist Caitlin O'Connell conducts her research.

MUSTH: a state of heightened sexual excitement and aggressive behavior in bull elephants.

NIGHT VISION EQUIPMENT: light-intensifying tools to help scientists see at night.

PACHYDERM: informal term used for large mammals such as hippos and elephants.

PACINIAN CORPUSCLES: vibration-sensitive cells found in an elephant's feet and trunk.

PAN: a shallow clay depression in the earth that holds water—sometimes seasonally, sometimes year-round.

PLANTHOPPERS: tiny insects that communicate by vibrating plants with their limbs.

RUMBLE: a common way elephants vocalize to communicate with one another.

SAVANNAH: a hot grasslands area with scattered trees, which alternates between dry and rainy seasons.

SEISMIC SIGNALS: one way animals communicate by making objects in their environment vibrate, such as the ground.

TESTOSTERONE: a hormone that bull elephants produce in large quantities when they're in musth.

TRUMPET: a loud, bellowing sound elephants make when they're anxious or attacking.

TRUNK: a long, tubelike appendage comprising an elephant's upper lip and nose.

TUSKS: an elephant's elongated incisor teeth, which are used as tools and weapons, and to lift objects.

WATERHOLE: an opening in the ground where rainwater collects.

68

SELECTED SOURCE NOTES

Caitlin O'Connell, Ph.D., ecologist, author, professor, and co-founder of Utopia Scientific; Timothy Rodwell, M.D., Ph.D., M.P.H., physician, photographer, and cofounder of Utopia Scientific; Joyce Poole, director, ElephantVoices; Colleen Kinzley, general curator, Oakland Zoo, Oakland, California; *The Elephant's Secret Sense: The Hidden Life of the Wild Herds of Africa* by Caitlin O'Connell (Free Press, 2007); "Four Ears to the Ground: For an Elephant, the Foot May Be a Powerful Listening Device," by Alan Burdick, *Natural History* magazine, American Museum of Natural History, April 2002; "Seismic Communication a Growing Field of Study," by Jeff Rice, National Public Radio, June 20, 2007; *Elephants,* by Joyce Poole (Voyageur Press, 1997); "Mammals: Elephant," San Diego Zoo Animal Bytes, www.sandiegozoo.org; "The Delinquents: A Spate of Rhino Killings," *60 Minutes II,* 1999; "Elephants' Toes Get the Message, Study Finds," by Colin Nickerson, *Boston Globe,* June 28, 2007; "African Elephant Program Factsheet," U.S. Fish & Wildlife Service; "Ivory Poaching at Critical Levels: Elephants on Path to Extinction by 2020?," University of Washington, *ScienceDaily,* August 1, 2008; "An Elephant Crackup?" by Charles Siebert, *New York Times,* October 8, 2006; "Elephant Breakdown," by G. A. Bradshaw, Allan N. Schore, Janine L. Brown, Joyce H. Poole, and Cynthia Moss, *Nature* 433, February 24, 2005.

INDEX

Page numbers in **bold** type refer to photographs.

Also by Donna M. Jackson:

Extreme Scientists

★ "The many excellent, color photos portray these adventurers as scientists intently focused on their work, though sometimes in unusual or unusually beautiful surroundings. . . . Fascinating."

—*Booklist,* starred review

ER Vets

An Orbis Pictus Honor Book

An ASPCA Henry Bergh Children's Book Award Honor Winner

★ "Well-researched and well-written, *ER Vets* is an engaging book on a hot topic."

—*School Library Journal,* starred review

The Bug Scientists

Winner, Parent's Guide to Children's Media Award

NSTA-CBC Outstanding Science Trade Book for Children

★ "The much maligned world of insects becomes fascinating in this latest entry in the excellent Scientists in the Field series."

—*Booklist,* starred review

The Wildlife Detectives

NSTA-CBC Outstanding Science Trade Book for Children

"A book that will be welcomed by fans and anyone who cares about animals."

—*Booklist*